Pebble® Plus

GREAT ASIAN AMERICANS

Yo-Yo Ma

by Stephanie Cham

CAPSTONE PRESS
a capstone imprint

Pebble Plus is published by Capstone Press,
1710 Roe Crest Drive, North Mankato, Minnesota 56003
www.mycapstone.com

Library of Congress Cataloging-in-Publication Data
Names: Cham, Stephanie.
Title: Yo-Yo Ma / by Stephanie Cham.
Description: North Mankato, Minnesota : Capstone Press, [2018] | Series:
   Great Asian Americans
Identifiers: LCCN 2017044060 (print) | LCCN 2017044739 (ebook)
ISBN 9781515799788 (eBook PDF)
ISBN 9781515799573 (hardcover)
ISBN 9781515799726 (pbk.)
Subjects: LCSH: Ma, Yo-Yo, 1955—Juvenile literature. | Cellists—United
   States--Biography—Juvenile literature. | Chinese
   Americans—Biography—Juvenile literature.
Classification: LCC ML3930.M11 (ebook) | LCC ML3930.M11 C4 2018 (print) | DDC
   787.4092 [B] –dc23
LC record available at https://lccn.loc.gov/2017044060

Editorial Credits
Abby Colich, editor; Juliette Peters and Charmaine Whitman, designers;
Morgan Walters, media researcher; Kathy McColley, production specialist

Photo Credits
ASSOCIATED PRESS: OSAMU HONDA, 13; Getty Images: Bettmann, 9, Bill Johnson, 7, Frans
Schellekens, 11, Hiroyuki Ito, 17, ImageCatcher News Service, 19, Jim Spellman, 21, Paul Morigi,
15, The Washington Post, Cover; Shutterstock: Attitude, design element throughout, j avarman,
(pattern) design element throughout, most popular, design element throughout, yari2000, 5

Note to Parents and Teachers

The Great Asian Americans set supports standards related to biographies.
This book describes and illustrates the life of Yo-Yo Ma. The images support
early readers in understanding the text. The repetition of words and phrases
helps early readers learn new words. This book also introduces early readers
to subject-specific vocabulary words, which are defined in the Glossary
section. Early readers may need assistance to read some words and to use
the Table of Contents, Glossary, Read More, Internet Sites, Critical Thinking
Questions, and Index sections of the book.

Printed and bound in the USA.
010771S18

Table of Contents

Childhood and Cello

Yo-Yo Ma was born in 1955.

He lived in Paris, France.

His parents were from China.

Yo-Yo began to play cello at age 4.

1955
born on October 7
in Paris, France

1959
begins playing
cello

Paris, France

Yo-Yo took cello lessons. He went to schools for music. He played his first concert at age 5. He and his family moved to New York in 1962.

1960
plays first concert

1962
family moves to New York

Yo-Yo and his sister

Yo-Yo finished high school in 1971.
He was only 15. He could have
played cello full-time. But he wanted
to learn about other things.
He began college in 1972.

1971
graduates from
high school

1972
begins college

A Life of Music

After college Yo-Yo played cello
full-time. He made his first album
in 1977. He played music others
had written. Soon he began
to write his own music.

1977
records
first album

Yo-Yo usually played classical music.

In 1991 he began to play other kinds.

He made a jazz album. He played

folk music. He learned about music

from around the world.

1991
begins playing new
styles of music

Spreading the Music

Yo-Yo wanted to teach music
to children. He taught at
music festivals. He gave classes.
He played on children's TV shows.

1955   1959   1960   1962   1971   1972   1977   1991

In 1998 Yo-Yo began

the Silkroad project. It uses music

to bring people together. Its musicians

go to schools. They work with teachers.

They bring music to more students.

1998
starts Silkroad
project

Yo-Yo has won many awards.
In 2001 he received the National
Medal of Arts. He received the
Presidential Medal of Freedom
in 2010. He has won 18 Grammys.

2001	2010	2017
receives National Medal of Arts	receives Presidential Medal of Freedom	wins 18th Grammy

1955   1959   1960   1962   1971   1972   1977   1991   1998

President Barack Obama gives Yo-Yo the Presidential Medal of Freedom.

Today Yo-Yo still makes music.
He has made more than
100 albums. He plays music
around the world.

1955   1959   1960   1962   1971   1972   1977   1991   1998   2001   2010   2017

Glossary

album—a collection of musical recordings

classical—a style of music rooted in the European tradition

festival—a group of musical or artistic events often held at the same time each year

folk—a style of music traditional to an area or culture

Grammy—an award for an achievement in the music industry

jazz—a style of music that features heavy drum rhythms and brass instruments such as trumpets, trombones, and saxophones

National Medal of Arts—the highest award in the United States given to artists

Presidential Medal of Freedom—one of the highest awards given by the president of the United States

Read More

Guillain, Charlotte. *Jobs if You Like…Music*. Chicago: Heinemann Library, 2013.

Nunn, Daniel. *Instruments and Music*. Chicago: Heinemann-Raintree, 2012.

Shea, Therese. *Yo-Yo Ma: Classical Musician*. Exceptional Asians. New York: Enslow, 2016.

Internet Sites

Use FactHound to find Internet Sites related to this book.

Visit *www.facthound.com*

Just type in 9781515799573 and go.

Super-cool stuff! Check out projects, games and lots more at **www.capstonekids.com**

Critical Thinking Questions

1. Name two styles of music Yo-Yo plays.
2. What is one way Yo-Yo has helped bring music to others?
3. Name one award that Yo-Yo has won.
   Use the Glossary on page 22 to define that award.

Index